Jesus told a story about ten bridesmaids.

AF208284

They waited to meet the bridegroom with their lamps.

Five were foolish. They forgot to take oil.

Waiting for the bridegroom, they all fell asleep.

'The bridegroom is coming. Go out to meet him.'

The bridesmaids got up and started to light their lamps.

The foolish girls realised they had no oil.

While the
foolish
girls were
buying
oil, the
bridegroom came.

The wise girls went into the wedding with him.

The door was shut. The foolish girls were too late.

This story warns us to be ready to meet with the Lord. We need to be forgiven for our sins.